LINGERING MEMORIES

Alan Lun

Translated by Angela Lun

CONTENTS

FOREWORD

Alan is a personal friend of mine and a co-worker in Herald UK Christian Newspaper for more than a decade. We have worked together on many platforms in the London Chinese Christians arena. Hence it is my privilege to write a foreword for this wonderful life testimony of his.

It is a life testimony of someone who was born during a very difficult time, no less to call it an era of chaos in a country that has since troubled many souls. Alan describes every twist and turn in his life journey gently and calmly which, in reality, could have led him to a very sorrowful path if not for God's intervention. Readers will probably find and echo their similar experiences in Alan's multiple encounters with God. It is therefore very encouraging to read this book.

Alan and his wife are thankful to God, and are determined to pass on their blessings, which I believe is the reason why he wrote. May Alan's life, and ours too, shine for HIS glory, and bring hope into a world full of despair.

Rev Dr Vincent Aun

FOREWORD

I consider reading other people's life stories, even better if they are auto-biographies (ghost-written or not), as a perfect investment of time. You practically live their entire life in hours and learn from their invaluable experience but without paying the price of going through the ups and downs.

It just occurs to me that I have known Alan for almost 30 years. He has always impressed me as a sincere and kind-hearted person who devoted much of his time to his family. Our life paths crossed when I taught at his son's school in London back in 1996. He invited me to stay at his home before I could find a place to live, in fact he eventually helped locating my first ever home in this city.

Despite the fact that we lost contact after some years, it must be the Lord's will that I came across his testimony in the Herald UK. I am intrigued by his experience and encounters which to be honest I was not aware of before and glad that he decides to write his autobiography.

I trust that we can all learn something from Alan, and his story is a living proof of the Lord's work among us.

Dr Raymond Tang
Educational Psychologist (UK)
Barrister (HK)

PREFACE

This book is about my life experiences. It describes my life journey, especially in Chapter 30 "God's Goodwill over the Course of My Life". I dedicate this book to God, my Heavenly Father. He has not only created me but has watched over me for over three quarters of a century. May He continue to empower my fingers; protect my brain from degeneration; maintain my ability to think and remember, to offer the rest of my life for His use. I would like to put this on record.

This book is also dedicated to my beloved wife Angela, who has shared my joys and sorrows for forty-eight years. She also translated the Chinese original of "Lingering Memories" into this book for me. In my gratitude, I dedicate this book to her to commemorate our 48th wedding anniversary.

This book also fulfils my life-long wish. Reading and writing are my hobbies and habits. In my lifetime, I express my heart with my hand to leave myself some "collections from the heart". If my Heavenly Father permits this book to be published, all proceeds will go to Herald UK to support their ministry.

Thanks to Rev Vincent Aun and Dr Raymond Tang for their Foreword, to Angela for translating this book for me, and to my son Ira for his proof-reading.

Alan Lun
2022

Chapter 1 Untimely Birth

I was born in tumultuous times. Hong Kong was already in its third year under the Japanese army's rule during World War II. The human misery and suffering in the city had to be experienced to be believed. Mother later told me that, as soon as the Japanese occupied Hong Kong, they imposed press censorship, and newspapers were merged or suspended. The Allied forces began bombing Hong Kong. People were killed by the bombs; or slaughtered; or drowned whilst fleeing; or hungry and helpless, starved to death on the streets. Corpses were everywhere. The horrors too harrowing to witness; the suffering unspeakable.

Due to fuel shortage, electricity supply was suspended for a month. As a result, all trams stopped running, causing traffic inconvenience. Moreover, the Japanese military police often imposed curfew from 6 pm, and Hong Kong suddenly plunged into darkness, like a ghost town. Food supply was severely inadequate, and citizens had to be rationed rice certificates in order to purchase this staple food. Unscrupulous merchants were hoarding to drive up prices. Most citizens were unemployed and had to pawn their gold, silver, jewellery and valuable clothes in exchange for money to buy food.

Hong Kong is surrounded by sea, and refugees could be seen everywhere. The Japanese military police used boats to carry them to a remote island to fend for themselves. The refugees discovered that there were no indigenous inhabitants, no farming or food production. It was unsuitable for human habitation. On their arrival, the refugees found that the place was a dead end. The deserted island was full of skeletons and devastation. It was utterly terrifying. Some of them tried to escape by swimming, but drowned halfway due to exhaustion. Those who stayed on the island either starved to death, or robbed others when they heard the sound of fighting.

The restaurant where Father worked closed down, so he was idle at home, smoking all day long. His two wives (men were allowed to have more than one wife at that time) had to earn a living by peddling in Cochrane Street in Central. "Big Aunt" sold haberdashery, while Mother styled beauty-conscious women's hair and removed their facial hair. These were their only skills to make a living, working from one day to the next. Sometimes they couldn't even get a single customer in a day – life was tough.

One day, two Japanese soldiers came. They each had a rifle with a bayonet attached to the end of the barrel. One rushed fiercely towards Mother, who wasn't quick enough to make way or bow down. He yelled at Mother to stand still, and slapped her in the face. Mother quickly backed off, apologising, saluting and bowing frantically. Only then did the soldiers take off. After they had gone, passers-by noticed Mother was pregnant, carrying me. They remarked how lucky she was. If the soldier turned his rifle on Mother and stabbed her belly with the bayonet, he would have taken two lives, and I wouldn't have been born into this world.

I was finally born. Mother had a small build, and I was even smaller, crying weakly. I wasn't strong enough to suck the breast milk when fed, so Mother had to smear some cooked rice water around my mouth to keep me alive. I was malnourished and skin and bones, too weak to even lift my limbs. At that time, many Hongkongers fled to Mainland China to escape the war. Father decided to follow the exodus up north, ending up in Guangzhou.

There we had an aunt living in the ancestral house, where we found shelter. After being fed with sweet potato paste, I gained some strength. I couldn't help feeling sad and cried when I felt hungry.

Chapter 2 Childhood

After the fall of Hong Kong in 1942, there was a food shortage. More than 450,000 Hongkongers fled to Guangzhou, a large city in southern China. Unfortunately Guangzhou also fell under the control of the Japanese Imperial Army, who burned, killed, raped and looted. A severe drought hit Guangdong in 1943, and agriculture failed, leading to starvation and corpses lying around, with no-one to bury them. Moreover, anti-Japanese activities flared up everywhere, so the Japanese army imposed strict measures to suppress the guerrillas. On August 15, 1945, Japan surrendered. Guangzhou is the capital and seat of the municipal government of Guangdong Province. It has a long history of 2,200 years and is the birthplace of Southern China's culture. It is the hub of prosperity and modern Chinese cultural development. The local dialect is Cantonese, which is very similar to that of Hong Kong, so citizens can communicate with each other without problems.

We fled from Hong Kong to Guangzhou, saving our family of five, and lived in our ancestral house in the area of Xiguan. The economy was very sluggish that year, and people struggled to earn a living. Dad called on his former employer and found a job at his restaurant, with a salary barely enough to sustain the family. After years of war and chaos, agricultural development was slow. Coupled with the lack of efficient transport, supply of produce in the Pearl River Delta, such as rice, vegetables, fruits, and sugar cane, was sparse and expensive. Industrial development was struggling. The handicraft industry was relatively developed, with Foshan's ceramic industry and art well known across the nation.

The ancestral house was located in the alleys of Wenchang South Road, a busy part of Guangzhou. The building was more than 50 years old. Other than a bedroom and a living room on the ground floor, the attic was only half as big as the ground floor, but also had a living room and a bedroom. A large wooden bed was added to the ground floor living room, and there was an indoor well in front of it for drinking, cooking and washing. There was a small kitchen at the back for cooking, baths and even toileting, with little regard for hygiene. The main door was a wooden folding one with a rolling wooden fence behind the door to prevent me and my sister from getting out of the house without the adults knowing. It also served to prevent thieves from breaking in. The house was small but had everything we needed.

When this new-born baby – me, the first boy in the house – was born, the whole family were overjoyed. When Mother cradled me in her arms, my soft body snuggled close to her. She played with my little hands, and my eyes turned to her face. Father hugged me and my sister leaned over to kiss the back of my hand. I felt so sweet – what a heart-warming portrait of family bliss!

On the other hand, when my parents brought me into the world, I had to face many uncertainties as I grew up. After the war against the Japanese ended in 1945, the daily life of Guangzhou citizens did not return to normal. Father had to shoulder the financial responsibility of the family. Prices fluctuated wildly from day to day, and the family struggled to make ends meet, not to mention saving up for the children's education in future.

Father had to work hard to put food on the table, while Mother stayed home to take care of my sister and me, as well as doing housework. With the financial constraints, the picture of family joy was no longer there, and the smiles disappeared from my parents' faces. To add to our misfortune, my aunt died from a sudden illness at a very young age. Her last wish was for me, her toddler nephew, to perform the traditional funeral rituals as her next of kin. It never rains, but it pours!

Chapter 3 Childhood Joy

When I was about five years old, I would roam the streets. There was no prescribed school age in those days, so rather than being idle at home, with Mother's permission, I would play with neighbours' children in the open space on the streets. Someone stole water from the fire hydrant and broke the faucet, and water splashed everywhere. We were like birds escaping from a cage, chattering and screaming, and innocently started playing around the faucet. We held hands in the water and, the moment the pillar of water stopped, we rushed across a wall of water together. The water inside the wall sprayed one wave after another, and we would run towards the gap between waves. There were many of us playing in a small space: we ran from side to side, back and forth, laughing and shouting, falling over each other – weaving a picture of water-splashing fun. Although this man-made rain hit my head and body, it was absolutely exhilarating.

It was a clear afternoon, and the sun, initially shy behind the clouds of white on blue, emerged like a baby's head from its mother, eager to catch a sight of this enchanting Earth. I didn't understand at that time but in retrospect, maybe mothers back then had to work hard all day long so couldn't spend any happy moments with their children. Every morning Mother had to go to the market to buy groceries, and I would play hide-and-seek with neighbours' children in the streets, or the "eagle-and-chicks" game. One child would play the eagle, another the hen, the rest would be her chicks. Before the game starts, all the chicks must hide behind the hen (hands on the shoulder of the chick in front). The eagle tries to catch the chicks that can't keep up with the hen. Any chicks caught will be out, until all the chicks are caught and the eagle wins. If no chicks are caught, the hen wins.

Toys are children's angels, and are exclusive possessions of lucky children born today. Back then, what were our toys? We would throw pebbles up in the air and then try to catch as many pebbles as we could in one hand. Whoever finished with the most pebbles would be the winner. Or we would use a thick wire to make a hook, hook it onto a metal ring from a broken wooden tub, and roll it along the street. Or with the neighbours' children, each would take a coin, roll it up a slanting wooden board with a brick under it. Whoever could roll the farthest would pick up his coin and throw it at another player's coin. If his coin hits the target, he wins and could keep both coins. Although the toys were all home-made or ready-made, they could be great fun to play with.

I grew up in Guangzhou. At that time, I was innocent and lively. I would run around outside the house with my neighbours' children every day, and would only go home when I was tired and hungry. After my younger sister was born, Mother had no time to take care of me. Once my cousin and I went for a swim in Liwan and became very tanned, and only dragged my exhausted body home well past dinner time. Mother had been worried about me, fearing I had been kidnapped. When she saw me looking like a lobster, she was so furious that she treated me to a good lashing, and no dinner for me that evening!

There were even more absurd events. Once, I walked to the Wen Wu Temple with my neighbours' child. Emulating Liu Bei, Guan Yunchang, and Zhang Fei, the 3 heroes in the Chinese historical novel "Romance of the Three Kingdoms", we knelt before the two gods Wen and Wu and became oath brothers. In retrospect, Chinese folk idol worship actually had two gods: "Wen" (civil) and "Wu" (military). If Liu Bei could be named a civil god, then wouldn't Guan Yunchang be a military god? Times have changed: I wonder if this oath brother is still alive? If so, we are so old and grey that we won't recognize each other anyway!

As those old childhood dreams emerge in my heart one after another, I miss the children in my neighbourhood, my cousins and oath brother. I love the pebbles, the home-made hook, iron rings and copper coins. I have never learned to swim, but the childhood joy has deeply imprinted happy and unforgettable memories in my heart.

Chapter 4 The Three-Anti & Five-Anti Movements

1949 saw the founding of New China. The initial establishment of a social aid system helped a large number of the unemployed and poor in Guangzhou, and brought new hope and social stability. Unfortunately, good times never last. In 1951, in the name of anti-corruption, the "Three-Anti Movement" launched a purge campaign against the private business community across the country. Guangzhou, being one of the developed coastal industrial and commercial areas, was no exception. Many capitalists and merchants were accused of corruption, condemned and paraded in the streets. At a very young age, I witnessed the condemned being tied up, kneeling on a large lorry with a wooden sign on their back listing their crimes. Red flags were flown on the vehicle and revolutionary songs were broadcast. There were men and women on the lorry beating gongs and drums to stoke the fervour, publicly denouncing the crimes of those kneeling down. After conviction, their fate would be detention in labour camps. This was a great shock to social and economic development at the time.

During the annual Grave-Sweeping Festival in 1951, Mother and I went to the barren cemetery to pay homage to our ancestors. There was a row of houses at the bottom of the hill. On the nearby hill, several militiamen with rifles and long sticks in their hands were directing a group of prisoners from the labour camp to excavate the hill, remove rocks and deserted tombstones to flatten the area. Tombstones were used to lay the steps of the passage.

Split rocks were taken on the spot to make up for any material shortage. Most of the prisoners were not young; they looked emaciated and exhausted, wearing flimsy sweatshirts or half-naked. They were working hard and sweating, using their hoes to remove weeds and tree trunks all over the hill. Coming down the hill, I saw the prisoners by the wooden fence. They were overjoyed to see leftover pig fodder washed down from upstream. They flocked across the passage to the stream, scooped up the polluted water and fodder with their hands into their mouths to relieve their hunger. Who can forget such indifference and sadness of the world!

In 1952, after the " Three-Anti Movement" came the "Five-Anti Movement". This also targeted the bribery in private industrial and commercial organisations, and launched a purge campaign among capitalists in these organisations. Many of them were condemned, convicted of serious crimes and sentenced to death. Again, it was the annual Grave-Sweeping Festival. There was a wall in the wilderness for executing prisoners who had been sentenced to death, and it happened to be execution time. Three blindfolded prisoners stood against the wall, one in the centre and one on each side of the wall with red flags flying. There were six soldiers from the People's Liberation Army: three half-kneeling in the front row, and three standing behind them. The officer read out the prisoners' convicted crimes, then gave the order. Several gunshots were heard. The prisoners fell to the ground, their brains spilling. One did not die instantly, and a soldier in the back row fired one shot to finish him off. The execution shocked me at a very young age – it is still vivid and unforgettable to this day.

The "Three-Anti and Five-Anti Movements" forced many capitalists and merchants into labour camps or execution. Some cases might be unjust, false or mistaken. Many suspects who couldn't withstand the persecution committed suicide, and the bourgeoisie across the country declined. This was a serious blow to the economy of every region. In view of this, the authorities revised the policy and ordered the end of these two social movements in October 1952.

Chapter 5 Initial Education

E very young child has to learn to walk. Imagine a child crawling on the floor towards a sofa, an armchair or a table, and then supporting his/her upper body with his/her legs, slowly getting up, taking the first step in his/her life. Unfortunately, when the child tries the second step, he/she may become unsteady and fall over. However, the child is undeterred, and will keep trying. With his/her body straightened up, he/she can stand up again and complete the remaining steps of this learning process. However, with mothers who push their babies around in strollers until the age of two or three, their children will take longer to learn to walk during their developmental stage.

Education is no exception. I didn't have the opportunity to go to school until I was seven. The private school was a small classroom with a few small tables and stools, a small blackboard, and a so-called teacher in his sixties. On my first day at school, a few children older than me were sitting in the classroom. An uncle accompanied me, carrying a lantern, a basket of sponge cakes and cooked eggs which had been dyed red (symbolising good luck). Uncle distributed these to the whole class to celebrate the start of my schooling together. I can still remember Uncle holding my little hand, picking up the writing brush, and copying the six basic Chinese characters for beginners in the exercise book. This completed the ceremony, and he carried the lantern, the leftover sponge cakes and eggs, and took me home.

Children are cute, lively, and funny, although their family

background and environment in which they grow up may be different. They may be naive and talk endlessly, but can be strong-willed and stubborn. Although I lived in poverty as a child, I always had a bright smile. I was innocent and lively, never dishonest.

One time in class, when the teacher asked: "Who has never lied?", most of the students raised their hands. He asked us again: "Those who have lied but raised their hands – haven't they lied to their teacher? They are deceiving themselves also." He told us that when we wash our face in the morning, we look at ourselves in the mirror and we are so ugly. To this day, I still remember the teacher's reproach, deeply etched in my heart.

Parents have ardent expectations for their children's education, but unfortunately not all of them spend enough time with their children during their development. My father would still be asleep when I went to school, and I would be in bed when he came home from work at night. Father and son should be very close, but sadly we hardly saw each other! It is true that the burden of life and the pressure of work could be overwhelming. Faced with the next generation who would shoulder the responsibility of tomorrow's world, all parents look forward to their children living more comfortably and achieving more than their parents did. Time spent together is much more precious – no money or material gifts can compensate for lost time and company. Loving care is better encouragement than screaming reproach and physical punishment. Dear parents: let us try to improve, and help and guide our younger generation. Together we can create a brighter future for them!

Chapter 6 Leaving My Hometown

After Hong Kong was liberated, the British Hong Kong Government resumed its rule. The British searched for food and other materials from all over Asia and shipped them to Hong Kong. Hongkongers who fled to the mainland to escape the war earlier returned with their family, young and old. Father heard that not only was Hong Kong restored to its previous conditions, but that its social welfare and education systems had been reformed and improved. So he and Big Aunt went back to Hong Kong to resume his former career and finally settled down.

Mother, my younger sisters and I still lived in the ancestral house in Guangzhou, but after experiencing the Three-Anti and Five-Anti Movements, even Hong Kong people who were not capitalists or merchants heard of the changes and had concerns about the new Chinese regime, and returned to Hong Kong. Moreover, schools and organisations in China were all taken over by the new government, and all private and religious schools had since disappeared. As a result, many educational institutions had to move to Hong Kong to resume classes.

I am the eldest son in my family. Father discussed with Mother and suggested that I should return to Hong Kong for education. I was only nine years old at the time. Although I was born in Hong Kong, I was displaced. After the fall of Hong Kong, I fled to Guangzhou to escape the ravages of war and spent my happy childhood days there. There was a young neighbour and good friend Yu Goh. His mother and mine were close like sisters. I often went to his house to play and even stayed overnight. Yu Goh expressed deep sympathy for my situation and volunteered to tell Mother that he could take me to Shenzhen by train, and I could cross Luohu Bridge on my own. Mother and I relayed his suggestion to Father, who readily agreed. He sent his apprentice to pick me up at the waiting area on the British side of the border at Luohu. On the appointed day, I set off on my journey, to be reunited with my Dad who was working in Hong Kong.

There is a Chinese saying: "A man away from his homeland is worthless". I started my independent life. I still remember attending a primary school affiliated with an electrical engineering college. The school was located at the junction of Hollywood Road and Wyndham Street. I didn't even know the 26 English alphabets – pity the 9-year-old me! During the English class, my teacher was a Mr Che, in his 50s. He wore a white shirt, trousers, a tie, and elastic bands around his arms to keep his shirt sleeves up. I was in awe of him – he was such a gentleman. He patiently and earnestly advised me: "Go to St. Paul's English Evening School down the road to brush up on your English, then you can catch up with the class. Study hard."

Having obtained my parents' consent, I enrolled for the English evening class. On the first evening, I discovered that this was an evening English college for adults, and there were very few young students like me. I just sat down in the first row, too embarrassed to look around. After studying for two years, I caught up with the daytime primary school curriculum. Moreover, the standards of Chinese language and Mathematics in Mainland China had surpassed those in Hong Kong, so I won the favour of the teachers in these two subjects. When the results of the Primary School Certificate Examination were published, I achieved Grade A in all three subjects - Chinese, English and Mathematics. At that time,

Mother had returned from the mainland to Hong Kong with my younger sisters, so the family was happily reunited. Our head teacher Mr Nong paid a special home visit and praised me in front of Mother as a reward.

Mr Che and Mr Nong suggested that I should enrol in two prestigious schools on Hong Kong Island, namely St. Paul's Co-educational School and St. Paul's Boys' School. I passed the entrance exams and both schools accepted me, but Big Aunt objected: "It's useless to study in an English secondary school. We Chinese should learn Chinese". Meanwhile, Father had invested in the Chinese cuisine department of the Chung Sing Swimming Shed in Western District. Opposite the swimming shed was the Chung Sing Chinese Lower Secondary School. My parents didn't value English education so arranged for me to enrol there. I was young and unable to object. I didn't tell my primary school head teacher Mr Nong, feeling that I let down my English teacher Mr Che, who had high expectations of me.

Chapter 7 Applying For Bursary

T he lower secondary school campus was not huge, only three stories high. The ground floor housed the Primary 1 to Primary 3 classrooms, teachers' room and a basketball court outside the passageway for PE lessons. The middle floor contained the Primary 4 to 6 classrooms, with a combined room for music and arts. The top floor housed the classrooms for lower secondary school Grades 1 to 3, with a cleaners' resting-cum-storage room. Unsurprisingly, such a small campus could not attract outstanding teachers. On my first day at school, I got the impression that it was even smaller than the English evening school I attended while at primary school. It was really disappointing.

The mixed quality of teachers was a major factor in the school's inability to produce good students. As I reached my rebellious age, I started to stray away from my studies, and spent most of my days playing basketball in the sports hall. After school, I would go to the tuck shop at the Chung Sing Swimming Shed where Mother worked. With her permission, I took snacks from the shop. Next to the tuck shop was a stall, manned by a young lady, which rented out life-rings and swimsuits. One quiet afternoon when there were very few swimmers, Mother, not knowing that I couldn't swim, asked the young lady to look after me while I realised my long-time wish – a dip in the sea. The swimming channels were divided into shallow and deep areas, separated by a big bamboo for swimmers to hold on to take a rest. I happily changed into my swimming trunks, and was so excited that I jumped into the sea without waiting for the young lady. The water was much deeper than I thought, and I couldn't swim to the bamboo to grasp it. In an instant, I gulped two mouthful of sea water. I was half floating and sinking when the young lady jumped down and lifted my head and back out of the water. I was in shock. Seeing this, Mother asked the young lady to help me back to the swimming shed. From then on, I never had the opportunity to learn to swim again.

I muddled through the three years at Chung Sing. My English was deteriorating. Fortunately, my Chinese and Maths were good. After graduating from lower secondary school, I didn't have a clue where I was heading. I was fifteen years old. Father wanted me to inherit his cooking skills as a chef to work at his restaurant, and told Mother to buy work-clothes for me. I strongly opposed the idea and told my parents: "I want to continue my studies, not be an apprentice in the kitchen! Don't worry, I will find a way to be self-sufficient and complete my secondary education."

Cousin Tak Ying expressed sympathy for my situation. She was an intellectual and a scholar. She regularly wrote articles for The Overseas Chinese Daily's special column. She saw that the newspaper offered bursaries and encouraged me to apply. I was very excited and immediately took action. The next morning, I set off at 4 am while it was still dark, and was first in the queue outside the office entrance. When they opened at 9 am, I went in to get the application form. God didn't let me down. I got my bursary and was enrolled into my dream school – the famous Pui Ying Chinese Middle School.

Pui Ying was a Christian school. Although it was a Chinese secondary school, mathematics, physics and chemistry used English textbooks and were taught in Chinese and English. Due to the low standard of English taught during the three years of lower secondary education, I fell behind and had much catching up to do, so had to study hard. There were religious activities during the three years of secondary education. Their Director of Religion took us to United Church in Bonham Road to join their worship. We also had Religious Studies and read the Bible. Initially I regarded the Bible as a general subject, and only studied it for the exams. I was fortunate enough to attend a rally held by the American evangelist Billy Graham at the Hong Kong Stadium in 1962. At that time I was just joining the rally for fun, and was pleased to have passed the Religious Studies exam in the Hong Kong Certificate of Education Examination.

Chapter 8 A Dream Come True

Dreaming is an active process taking place in a person's sleep, and "a dream come true" is the fulfilment of a dream – a dream being transformed into reality. I had a dream when I was a teenager – to go to university. Looking around me, all my schoolmates' aspiration after graduating from secondary school was to progress to further studies. Their first choice was the University of Hong Kong, second choice being the Chinese University. At that time, my family was quite poor, and I was only able to complete secondary education with the aid of bursaries. It was inconceivable for me to go to university. Moreover, my father's stomach cancer diagnosis had been confirmed, and the financial burden of the family naturally fell on me as the eldest son.

The cruel reality of life forced me into the "university of society". Although I couldn't afford higher education for the time being, I still did my best to support my younger siblings to fulfil the aspiration that I myself couldn't achieve. It is comforting that my younger brother obtained a PhD, and my younger sister graduated from a college of education. My regret of not having been able to go to university led to a dream I was to pursue for much of my life. It became deposited and buried in my heart for 33 years. Work, part-time jobs, and evening studies filled my timetable. Due to the lack of academic qualifications, only diligence could make up for my deficiencies: I consoled myself with diplomas from off-campus courses. One evening when attending a class at the University of Hong Kong, I walked into the main entrance and stood there for 30 minutes, gazing at the university motto "Sapientia et Virtus" ("Wisdom and Virtue"). I looked up to the sky and asked, "God: Can you grant me this wish of going to university?"

During my years of searching for a way to go to university, I came across a book entitled "How To Get A Degree In Britain". I had found my treasure, and bought it at once without asking about the price. Not sure how many times I read that book! It gave me the drive, ignited my life, and illuminated my heart. "God! Can You grant me this wish?" This wish hovered in my mind. It was a flame that burned brightly in the back of my mind, and would not be extinguished. I migrated to the UK and God had not forgotten me, a prodigal son once educated under the influence of Christianity. His grace and kindness revived my dream of pursuing higher education. Can this be achieved? I asked again and again, "God! Can You grant me this wish?"

With my pastor's recommendation, I managed to do part-time work and regain the joy of studying. I studied English for three years and obtained a certificate. My English teacher at the college was an angel sent by God. He asked me, "Do you want to go to university?" I stroked my balding head and replied, "I'm an over-aged student. Is it possible?" He said, "Why not?" I had no answer. Under his patient guidance, I filled out the application form, choosing my subject. He also suggested that I apply for student allowance and loans. Like a toddler, I nervously took the first step.

I had been away from school for more than 30 years. After I finished secondary school in Hong Kong, I never had the opportunity to go to university. It was therefore amazing for me to succeed in my application as someone outside the expected age range for the average university student. As I only started applying before the January deadline instead of applying one semester earlier as required, my first choice of university and subject were full so I had to take the second choice. It seemed surreal to resume my studies after all these years. This was the dream of a middle-aged man in his 50s, like a student carrying his schoolbag, and once again unveiling the prelude to another stage in life. I would like to testify: had it not been my Heavenly Father's plan in my life, I would not have obtained a degree in psychology in 2001. He had guided my dream to a perfect conclusion. All in all, my dream was fulfilled not due to the right time, the right place or the right people, but by the grace of a God who truly loves me.

Middlesex University

Chapter 9 Life On Campus

I was born in Hong Kong, spent much of my childhood in Guangzhou, and return to my birthplace Hong Kong at the age of 9. After I migrated to the UK, London became my second home. When I first came to the UK, I stayed at a friend's house in Cambridge. Every day I would run into students from different colleges of the University. I admired them for being able to attend a world-renowned university and felt ashamed of not being one of them. Inside the three-storey bookshop there, the shelves were filled with books on different subjects. For a book-worm in his 50s, all these only made me yearn even more for the opportunity to study at university.

Then my dream came true. The university I picked was not far from home, only half an hour's drive away. At the start of the induction week, I stepped into the university campus in London with great excitement and turbulent emotions. I roamed around the spacious campus, taking in everything like a butterfly sipping nectar. Initially, I often found myself lost on my way to and from the classrooms. It was amazing listening to lectures, sitting high up in the lecture theatre with over 200 seats.

The library was located on the second floor of an L-shaped building. The basement housed the computer room, student group meeting room, screening room, and the checkout desk. There was a wealth of books in the library. If you bury your head in the collection of books, you will discover that your knowledge is so shallow, merely a drop in the ocean, and you can't read all the books in a lifetime. Doesn't this prove that there is no limit to learning! The library didn't open until 8:30 am. In order to get a parking space, I would arrive at the campus before 8 am, go to the student cafeteria and enjoy a refreshing cup of tea, and get to know some new students.

Then began a very rewarding life on campus. Professors and lecturers recommended a large number of reference books during the lectures, so immediately after class I would go to the library to find the required books and other relevant journals. As I was still working part-time on weekends in my first year at university, despite my hard work, I failed two modules: Introduction to Psychology and English Language & British Institutions.

This was a very heavy blow and I felt numb. Eventually I gathered my wits somewhat, and still feeling depressed, went to ask the professor for advice on how to remedy the situation. He asked me in detail about my daily routine. I answered truthfully: part-time jobs on Friday, Saturday and Sunday; classes from Monday to Thursday. Except for meal times, the rest of the day was for studying, homework, studying, and homework again. To which he responded: "You spend too much time studying, exhausting your energy. Sometimes the more you study, the less you benefit." It was then that I realised I had been attempting to drill knowledge into my brain without digesting or assimilating it. At the beginning of the second semester, I quit my part-time job, adjusted my work and rest schedule, re-sat the two failed exams, and became a full-time university student.

Life on campus also had a relaxing side. For example, I could chat with students from different faculties in the morning and afternoon, and to meet some new students. It was an enjoyable experience, in which I also got to improve my English communication skills. One day I found an elderly man walking among the students with the help of a cane. I invited him to sit next to me, asked him what he would like to drink and bought him a cup of coffee. I learned that he was amblyopic and studied Chinese medicine. He was approaching 70, more than ten years my senior. I was in awe of him. At his age, most Chinese would have retired long ago. I asked him why he chose this subject, and he replied, "It's my interest!" I felt really humbled.

Chapter 10 Theological Studies

In 2003 God called me to follow in His footsteps. In order to make me a useful vessel for Him, He called me to study theology. In retrospect, I was willing to obey God's instructions because I enjoy studying, and theology is the pursuit of biblical knowledge. Truth is a treasure hidden in the Bible. Theology is the interpretation of this truth, and the Bible is the life-changing word of God. As a lay Christian, I had enjoyed church life for six years, and it was time to respond to God's great love. I was called by Him, chosen by Him to become a believer. Although I am not Jewish and was never circumcised, I was baptised in 1999 and accepted into God's family. What an honour it is to be a child of God! Therefore I readily agreed to take up theological training at the Chinese Overseas Christian Mission (COCM) Bible College.

The Chinese have a history of five thousand years. In the early days, they had little chance of coming into close contact with Christianity. They had no relationship with Jesus Christ at all; there was no God in their hearts, and there was no hope of everlasting life in their world. Theology has taught me that the Jews (or Israelites) were God's chosen people. God made a covenant with them and promised that the Lord would pour out His Spirit on their descendants and bless their children. The Chinese were in fact Gentiles. However, God's salvation is truly wonderful. He sent His beloved Son Jesus Christ to come into the world as a man. Jesus acted as the mediator to restore a true and beautiful relationship between God and man. Jesus is the way and, through His death and resurrection, we can be reconciled with God. This is the key meaning of the Christian faith. Studying theology, I found that in this endless and eternal universe, there is a loving, compassionate God. He knows us, and in His infinite love, through His Son Jesus' precious blood, accomplished His salvation for us who had drifted away from Him.

Knowing God is the biggest gain in my life. By faith I trust in the King of Peace. Through His sacrifice on the cross, He reconciled man to God. The spiritual wall has been demolished by the death of Christ. I am in Christ Jesus and my body was nailed to the cross with Jesus as a living sacrifice to God. At the same time, I was moved by the Holy Spirit and became a new creation. I hope that after being born again, I will have God's disposition and become more and more like the Lord Jesus Christ. If I study theology, accept the teachings of the lecturers, and study the truths of the Bible, I have to break away from my old self and behaviour of the past, and renew my mind. This new man was reformed according to God's will, in God's plan. I need to equip myself for His Kingdom.

As my theology studies at the COCM Bible College were mainly via distant learning, it took me five years to complete the three-year course, on completion of which I graduated in 2007. I was awarded a certificate by Dr. Rifeng Lin, Dean of COCM Bible College, and endorsed by Ms. Wang Guangxia, Director-General of COCM. Although the course was mainly distant learning, I had to attend two weeks of on-site classes in Milton Keynes during the summer break. After the Global Enrichment Theological Seminary, based in the US, set up their branch in London (GETS UK), I studied some of my favourite courses in 2008 and 2011.

Chapter 11 Novice In Love

In Hong Kong during the 1960s, accounting firms had to have an accountant licence to practise. Exports from Hong Kong required export certification documents, which in turn required costing, to certify that the goods were produced in Hong Kong, and not re-exports originally produced in Mainland China. There were also quota restrictions. As a result, every export certificate had to be endorsed by an accountant before being accepted by the Trade and Industry Department so that the manufacturer could export the goods. I was an apprentice learning from a senior accounting clerk as my mentor. There were no computers and we used abacuses for calculations. My monthly salary was a meagre HK$200, from which $120 was spent on my younger siblings' education. Struggling to make ends meet, I also worked part-time in the evening as an accountant. For self-improvement, I studied accounting one evening per week.

On completion of the three-year apprenticeship, I worked there another year before switching to another audit firm. Although my salary had doubled, I was still struggling financially so took up two part-time jobs in the evening. After my daytime work, I would buy a bread roll to eat, and would not have dinner until I got home at 10 pm. During that period, I also sponsored a very motivated young man. Having myself had to rely on the Overseas Chinese Daily bursary to complete my secondary education, I felt empathy for him.

I still remember there was another audit firm next door. Our firm's and their firm's employees were friendly with each other and, being young people around the same age, we went on trips together from time to time. One year before Christmas, my colleague Jo's classmate Angela came to visit her, and gave her a calendar for the new year. When she came to use the telephone on my desk, I glanced at her and was struck by her beauty. I couldn't believe my eyes.

At home that night, I couldn't sleep, tossing and turning, thinking of her. Could she be my dream girl? Could this be love at first sight? I could only dream of such a pure and innocent girl. I made up my mind as to what to do. It transpired that Ah Yuen from the firm next door fancied Jo, so he and I planned trips and gatherings to create opportunities for ourselves. And through Jo's introduction, I finally met her classmate, the love of my dreams.

Back then, there were two students from the accounting faculty of the Polytechnic training in our audit firm and the one next door.

One of the trainees Miss So had her birthday around Christmas and invited us all to her birthday party at the Polytechnic. She also mentioned that it would be a dance party. As a novice in love, I neither knew how to dance, nor the social etiquette at a dance party, and I didn't know how to handle it. Ah Yuen assured me, "Fear not – I'll teach you. That evening, drink a little wine and be brave, and it will be fine." I followed his instructions. After work, Jo taught me some dance steps, and invited her classmates to the party, including Angela of course. That night, the two of us naturally became dancing partners, and I didn't leave her side for a minute.

The following year, we planned to travel with some colleagues and ex-classmates to Macau, where Angela's ex-classmate Laurinda came from. She had two flats there, one large and one small, and invited us to stay with her. We were overjoyed and readily agreed. I dug deep into my savings and bought a Japanese-made camera in order to take some group photos, hoping to capture my lover's image as a souvenir. When our ferry came out of Kap Shui Mun ("The Gate of Fast-Moving Water"), Angela felt nauseous on the choppy seas. Fortunately, I brought sea sickness pills to solve the problem. This seemed to have impressed her. When we arrived at the Macau pier, it was still dark. Everyone was in high spirits, clamouring to see the famous Lisboa Casino, and Angela was no exception. On arrival at the casino, we were given chips worth $25 per person to play at the slot machines. We both lost, but did not play on so avoided emptying our wallets!

Chapter 12 Tying The Knot

At the beginning when the world was created, God also created Adam, the ancestor of mankind. God said: "It is not good for man to live alone. I will create a woman for him that matches him." Thus God created Eve and established marriage. Thank God for creating my life partner and bringing us together. After three long years of dating, I proposed to the love of my life, and she agreed. In 1974, we finally tied the knot. New Year's Day was specially set as the wedding day, when we held a big banquet for relatives and friends. The first day of each year is our wedding anniversary. As it is a public holiday, it seems the whole world celebrates with us.

The wedding is still fresh in my memory. Regrettably it wasn't held in a church as neither party was a Christian yet. We were registered at the City Hall Marriage Registry and took our marriage oath there, "For better, for worse, for richer, for poorer, in sickness and in health, to love and to cherish each other, till death us do part." Witnessed by our loved ones, we completed the registration ceremony and became husband and wife. We became lifelong partners, forever and ever! We must stick to that oath and shoulder this sacred responsibility together faithfully.

After the New Year, we went on a 10-day tour of Taiwan for our honeymoon. The tour leader took care of us throughout the journey, and places of interest were everywhere. The most fascinating place was the Yehliu Geopark in Taipei, where we lingered and had photos taken together. The most awe-inspiring features were the mushroom-shaped rocks, eroded and formed by sea-water, strong winds and rain over the years into strange and fascinating shapes, many known for what they were said to resemble — the most famous one being the "Queen's Head". Due to the large number of tourists, we had to wait for more than half an hour to take pictures. After that, I found another double-mushroom-shaped rock resembling the "Lovers' Rock". I was deeply touched by it, and took lots of photos among these beautiful rocks — and some lovely memories with me.

The next day, we visited Yangmingshan National Park, another tourist attraction. The scenery along the way was beautiful and dazzling. It overlooked the Seven Star Mountains and the Milky Lake. Its beauty absolutely lives up to its reputation. According to the tour guide, most of the villas on Yangming Mountain were occupied by wealthy families. Those ideal homes were priceless. Then we travelled south along the route to Alishan in Chiayi. The song "Girls of Alishan" was made popular by singer Teresa Teng. "The mountain is green, the water is blue. The girls of Alishan are as beautiful as the water, and the young men of Alishan are as strong as the mountain!" The tour guide played this song on the coach, and everyone sang along and had a really great time.

Sun Moon Lake in Taichung is a place where the aborigines live. As we got off the coach, natives wearing ethnic costumes came to us selling handicrafts. Strolling through the mountain pass was most relaxing and enjoyable. The Formosan Cultural Village was a feast for the eyes. The Ami tribe's "Oath of Eternal Love" performance was especially meaningful for us newlyweds. The last stop was Kaohsiung, where the Zhongzheng Bridge spans the Love River. It was originally named to commemorate a couple who jumped into the river and died for their love. It became a tourist attraction after reports by the media. I hope that all lovers are able to eventually tie the knot, and not live a life of regrets.

Chapter 13 Visiting My Hometown

I n 1975, a year after I got married, I took my wife Angela to my hometown Guangzhou to visit my relatives. It was her first visit to the mainland. Although she spoke and wrote the same language, her cultural background was completely different. I remember when we were going through Shenzhen Customs, the officer asked what her job in Hong Kong was. She told him she was a secretary, and he asked: "What does a secretary do?" She replied: "I arrange work and meetings for my boss." The officer declared: "That's serving capitalists." She was stunned.

I hadn't visited my ancestral home for more than 20 years, and Angela was unaccustomed to the way of life there. It didn't have a bathroom, so we had to go to our good friend Yu Goh's house on a nearby street to take our bath. We received warm hospitality from relatives and friends. The lady who lived in my house was over a hundred years old and quite frail. She took one of the chickens they were keeping, and told her daughter-in-law to cook it for our dinner. We felt so indebted to them. After dinner, Angela told me she had never tasted such delicious chicken soup in her life, "Even the chicken bones taste great!" One day, Yu Goh's children showed us around tourist attractions in Guangzhou. In the zoo we saw over a thousand monkeys on the man-made hill, seeking bananas and other fruits from passers-by – we retreated and dared not go near!

During this trip, Angela and I went to my ancestral hometown Zhaoqing City to find my roots. The Seven Star Crags is a major tourist attraction in China. Legend has it that its seven peaks were left by Nüwa, the mother goddess of Chinese mythology after she repaired the Pillar of Heaven. As soon as we got off the coach, we were able to see the seven peaks and the lakes. We bought tickets to go inside the cavern in a small boat. There were stalactites and stalagmites everywhere, as well as carvings of beautiful ancient calligraphy on the rocks. In some places, we had to bend down in order to pass through. It was amazing to see all the rolling crags and peaks, lakes and mountains. I took lots of photos for the memory.

The most unforgettable thing for me was the name of the officer in charge of the Crags I saw on the notice board, which turned out to have the same family name as mine. We asked the Tourist Information Office how many people there were in this village with that family name. They replied: more than three hundred.

The Seven Star Crags is rightly renowned for having "the mountains of Guilin and the waters of Hangzhou", both places famous for their scenic beauty. We had a great day and returned home at sunset. It was a worthwhile trip: not only traveling and visiting relatives, but also fulfilling my dream of finding my roots.

We set off on our journey home the next day. There were many people passing through Shenzhen customs. The officer maintaining order suddenly divided the travellers into two queues, separating Angela and I. I was looking behind me to try to keep her within my sights, when the officer barked an order at me: "Show me your return permit." He then took my permit, and ordered me to follow him. I couldn't imagine what interest they could possibly have in me. We entered a room where he handed me over to another officer. The second officer barked another order at me, to open my luggage and separate the contents one by one. He then cut open the zipper and inner compartments with a blade; even my clothes and inside pockets were no exception.

Lastly he examined my camera. Seeing a roll of film, he asked me where I had been to take pictures. I told him about our visit to the Guangzhou Zoo and the Zhaoqing City one-day tour. He asked why I hadn't had the filmed developed. I replied, "I only returned to Guangzhou from Zhaoqing City yesterday evening, and the photofinishing shop was already closed. He told me to post the film back to Guangzhou before letting me go. After I had posted the package, I passed through customs and finally arrived at Luohu to be reunited with Angela, who had been waiting there for hours. It really felt like a lifetime had passed!

Chapter 14 At The Crossroads

I graduated from secondary school in 1963. Finding work in Hong Kong in the 1960s was hard – as the saying goes "graduation means joblessness". As my grades in the Hong Kong Certificate of Education Examination failed to reach the threshold for admission to the University of Hong Kong or the Chinese University, I had no hope of furthering my studies. At that time, Yu Goh had swum from the mainland to Hong Kong in 1962 to escape the famine. He was the one who took me to Shenzhen by train when I was 9; so when he finally reached Hong Kong, we were reunited after a long separation. I had just graduated and it was my summer vacation. As my future was undecided, I stayed with him for two months, and helped him with some handicrafts in my free time. After dinner we would go fishing by the pier. During holidays, we would go hiking together, and I would show him around famous tourist attractions in Hong Kong. We had endless things to talk about, and became very good friends.

Father was past his retirement age, but there were many hungry mouths to feed at home. My youngest brother was still in primary school. Father was diagnosed with stomach cancer during a check-up and had to seek medical help. Dr Yeung King Wong, husband of the famous Cantonese opera actress Fong Yim Fen, confirmed that it was terminal cancer, and nothing could be done. I had to shoulder the responsibility as the eldest son in the family, and my younger sister Ah Bing dropped out of school to work in the factory to support the family. Fortunately, Cousin Tak Ying, who taught at the Kowloon Chamber of Commerce Middle School, helped me secure a job as a teacher at their evening primary school. As I only finished secondary school, I couldn't teach at a secondary school. Through her introduction, I also became a full-time teacher at a primary school on Hong Kong Island during the day, and was registered with the Department of Education as a qualified teacher.

Most of the students in the evening class were young and had to work during the daytime. I remember a pair of twin sisters in the class. I was 19 years old, only a few years older than them. I admired their diligence and eagerness to learn. To encourage them to be physically and mentally healthy in order to have the energy to cope with their studies, I proposed a one-day trip to Red Plum Valley in Sha Tin during the weekend. They were overjoyed and readily agreed. I was in my early days as a teacher, and didn't know that I needed to obtain approval from the school before I could take students out. When the school found out, I was cautioned and, as a punitive measure, my contract was not renewed for the next year. I learned a hard lesson and regretted not having acted sensibly.

At the daytime primary school, there was a student who had little respect for teachers and often fell behind in his homework. I invited his parents to a meeting to try to understand their situation at home, but was bluntly rebuffed by his very protective mother. I felt deeply hurt and had to swallow my tears. I also felt indebted to Cousin Tak Ying for her love and kindness, thinking I had let her down, failing to meet her high expectation for me. I remember when I was in the fifth year of primary school, I aspired to be a teacher; I could find another teaching job. However, after careful consideration and having experienced the heavy responsibilities of a teacher, I no longer wanted to continue and decided to leave the ranks of educators.

Having learned from the painful experience, I went to my close friend Yu Goh to seek his advice: "I'm at a crossroads; which way should I go?" He was very sympathetic: "Teaching is a profession to be respected, and you would be negligent in the performance of your duties if you didn't discipline students who were stubborn and failing. If you feel wronged, you can't continue. You can pursue other careers. Anything you are interested in, give it a try." God didn't abandon me: it suddenly dawned on me that I had always been interested in maths. It so happened that my old landlord was a partner of an audit firm in Central District. There was a vacancy in his company and he invited me to attend an interview. As a result, my life turned a new page.

Chapter 15 Self-Improvement

I worked at two audit firms for 4 and 5 years respectively. During this period I continued to study in my spare time for self-improvement, including accountancy & finance ; business administration courses at The Hong Kong Management Association ; banking programme ; computing operation ; English and Business English courses organised by the British Council, and general psychology at the Hong Kong Baptist University's school of Continuing Education.

After graduating from secondary school, my 33 years of working in Hong Kong began with me joining an audit firm as an apprentice. It was a difficult start with a meagre salary, and I had to work part-time at night to make ends meet. The only thing I could do at the time was spur myself on to strive for progress. "When the going gets tough, the tough get going." I left the audit firm in 1973 and went to work for commercial firms. With my efforts I was able to gain the trust of my employers, and I worked as the Chief Accountant at five different companies over 33 years. The last company was comparatively larger, engaged in garment manufacturing, with factories in Sri Lanka and Bangladesh, and a liaison office in New York, USA. In the process from manufacturing to export sales, as the Financial Controller, I was responsible for allocating finance, issuing letters of credit for ordering materials, signing export documents, bank transfer to overseas factories, etc.

In 1992, I had to travel to Bangladesh to inspect the accounting and financial status of an overseas factory. At that time, Bangladesh was suffering from floods all year round, so before traveling I had to have various vaccinations to prevent infections, although I heard that there would be side effects such as gastrointestinal discomfort and hair loss. On arrival there, I saw what looked like a vast ocean and thought that I was at the seaside. It turned out that there was flooding everywhere. The water was ankle-deep, causing traffic chaos. What bothered me most was the mosquitoes flying out of the toilet, and poor hygiene was evident.

During my visit to the factory, it was clear that they were using child labour. Some of the boys and girls were only eleven or twelve years old, even the taller ones were only fifteen or sixteen. Of course, there were many adult female and male workers. The factory manager said, "They are lucky to be working here to help with their families' financial burden." I asked what their daily salary was. He said about US$1, with no overtime pay other than an apple or a banana as a reward. They must absolutely obey the overtime system or they would be fired. It's not surprising that today's human rights campaigners across the world are raising their concerns with buyers about the use of child labour by manufacturers in developing countries.

On my return flight back to Hong Kong, passengers were all seated and the time for departure had passed. At that moment, a limousine arrived on the tarmac and it was the prime minister of Bangladesh who got off. She was late due to a safety inspection. Although she was of course seated in first-class, it was a privilege to be travelling on the same plane and catch a glimpse of her, which was a pleasant surprise.

Chapter 16 Parenting Seminars

I n July 1996, I worked part-time at the Bishop Ho Ming Wah Chinese Centre as a Project Officer to promote a new series of "Formula of Parental Love" seminars. Back in 1994, when I was in Hong Kong, I completed a comprehensive parenting course run by Positive Living United Services (PLUS) and met their chairman, Professor C K Wong. He had hosted three series of "Formula of Parental Love" programmes on HKTVB, and gave videos of these to the Bishop Ho Ming Wah Chinese Centre as a gift. I compiled these into teaching materials for parenting children of different age groups: the first and second series called " Formula of Parental Love for Children", and the third series "Formula of Parental Love for Adolescents". I contacted the Association of Chinese Schools in Britain to let them know that I would be conducting seminars based on these teaching materials. The Association referred their member schools to these seminars, held at Chinese schools on Saturdays and Sundays for parents while their children were in class.

The idea of "Formula of Parental Love – Happy Families Come from Love" is that children are a gift to parents from God, and every parent loves their children, because God is love. A happy and complete family starts with parent-child relationship. The seminars aimed to help parents establish a close relationship with their children, cooperate with the school on their children's studies, understand their children's emotions and behaviour. The seminars were especially about conflicts between adolescents and their parents.   The seminars also helped parents to examine difficulties they were experiencing in their lives outside their relationship with their children, solve interpersonal and occupational problems, marriage and relationship with their spouse, finance, etc and how these affect their children. The parenting seminars helped parents to apply what they learned to achieve harmony in the family, with good results in all aspects of their children's lives.

With the help and promotion of the Chinese Schools Association and advertisements in the Sing Tao Daily, these seminars drew a good response. We had parents of children of different age groups from Chinese schools in many different regions attending, mostly for the children's series. In the more sizeable Chinese schools, the seminars were divided into classes and stages according to the parents' needs. These seminars taught them about parenting and how to encourage the development of healthy parent-child relationships. Through videos, handouts and workshops, we explored the difficulties encountered in nurturing and teaching children, which many parents found very helpful. The seminars lasted for three years, and were very popular among Chinese schools and Chinese families from many different areas, including Swansea in Wales. I was also invited by the Chinese Women's Association of Northern Rhine District and the Chinese Chamber of Commerce in Germany for ten days, to conduct parenting seminars in different German cities including Frankfurt and Cologne. The Chinese schools in Luxembourg were also very interested in the courses, and requested course materials and handouts.

In addition to part-time jobs and parenting lectures, I attended a training course provided by Parentline Plus at the London Open College Network, and obtained:

Credit Certificate: Introduction to Family & Childcare: Facilitation Training Qualification.

Chapter 17 Writing As
An Act Of Service

I love reading, and I think the saying "There is a house of gold in every book" is very true. A house of gold does not really mean there is a storage of gold, but that there are treasures in the book for you to discover, so you should make time for reading. We learn from a book by thoroughly understanding it and being inspired – not only getting knowledge from it, but through the book, experiencing our world and the human relationships therein. As the ancient saying goes: "Knowledge is understanding the world and handling relationships properly; a literary work is the lessons learnt from this experience". The treasures that can be found in a book are truly precious.

In 2006, Mrs Katie Chau, Director-General of the Chinese Christian Herald Crusades, came to the UK to hold a seminar in the Chinese Church in London (CCIL) in Hammersmith to recruit writers. She made it clear that their goal is to defend the biblical truth. However, their target audience is not only Christians in the church, but also non-Christians in the community, where they hoped to spread the gospel message, to honour God and be of benefit to people. After the training, I agreed to join as a writer.

In fact, I had begun writing for Herald Europe in 1997, and wrote my first article "A Christmas Like No Other". Years later, Herald UK branched out of Herald Europe. I joined Herald UK when the late sister Miuhan To was working on the preparations for its formation. We met regularly to plan the theme for each issue; division of responsibilities amongst co-workers: supplementary columns; articles on special topics; editorials; inviting columnists to contribute; editing; organising fellowships; Sunday promotions; monitoring work progress, etc. In the early stage, I also wrote theme articles and shared in editing work.

On one occasion, my wife and I visited the US headquarters of Chinese Christian Herald Crusades and met with Mrs Katie Chau again. She showed us around the building located near New York's Chinatown and their various editorial departments. She also told us that in every corner of the world, where there were Chinese, there was the Herald publication. The editorial work of Herald around the globe was coordinated from the headquarters. Most eye-opening for me was a small chapel on one of the floors for employees to worship and pray before starting work every morning. On a lower floor was a social service centre. As the headquarters were close to Chinatown, many Chinese gathered there every day. It provided a variety of activities, including counselling for autistic children. More than a dozen parents brought their children to join.

The Herald monthly is an invaluable Chinese publication. It is constantly exploring new directions, so there is a different topic every month. The supplementary columns are written by different authors with different styles for readers to choose from. Herald is a worldwide paper, free of charge.

Chapter 18 Voluntary Work

After obtaining my psychology degree and professional membership of the British Psychological Association, I joined the Chinese Mental Health Association (CMHA) as a volunteer to serve people in need and to gain work experience. Working in social care had been my long-time goal, and working with the CMHA allowed me to realise this goal. They provide mental health services to the Chinese community, focusing on service users' quality of life, encourage them to rebuild their confidence and integrate into society. CMHA employees include social workers, counsellors, medical consultants, etc, and all employees have professional qualifications. They seek to actively promote the mental health of Chinese in the UK, and they do this via different media — for example by regularly holding lectures and public seminars, contributing to magazine columns, and producing health pamphlets, television programmes and videos.

How should service users examine and deal with their mental health in order to heal their pain and strengthen their belief in themselves? "Health is priceless." Unable to find peace, people are often left feeling alone with their fears and sorrows, depression and troubles, deprived of joy. If we cannot quieten our minds, we may lose our appetite and lose sleep at night. If this condition continues, we will develop health problems which may affect our ability to work. However, if we can find peace in ourselves, there is much joy to be experienced. Peace can bring warmth and happiness to the family. Peace is indispensable in life. A good night's sleep is priceless, and peace in one's heart is precious.

With a joyful heart, we can face the world and other people with confidence and optimism. We can deal with any situation when our mind is calm. We face disappointment with hope, overcome depression with a positive mind, and persevere to the end.

To break through any psychological barrier, we inevitably must first face up to it, and actively find a way through. At this stage, instead of bemoaning our pain and loss, we can try to pick ourselves up and start moving forward again. Nothing can be gained by complaining about misfortunes and unhappy days. Feeling powerless and regret will only make us feel more frustrated, anxious, disappointed and overwhelmed. We must have the courage to go on and never give up.

How we regain our enthusiasm for life is a test of tenacity, perseverance and self-reliance in adversity. There is no harvest without hard work, and there is no hard work without harvest. In life, as long as we work hard, we will get results. A truly fulfilling life depends on our attitude towards suffering and being at ease with the world. A sense of crisis can be transformed into a sense of peace. Turn difficulties into opportunities; meet challenges with a smile. Such an enterprising spirit is the main driving force. Go all out and live a happy life.

As a psychological counsellor at the CMHA, I befriended clients first to gain their trust. Our relationship was one between friends, not between a psychologist and a patient. First, I would chat about their daily life, learn about their current situation, and ask them if they slept well recently, ate well and whether they needed to take any medication. After each question, I would listen attentively in order to learn about them. I would observe their appearance, emotions, speech, gestures and body language. These signals can show their health, emotional response, social behaviour, adaptability, prejudice, knowledge, and other characteristics. Appropriate counselling can be provided only after understanding the service user's needs. Conversation has the effect of easing the burden on the person's mind. I once visited a patient at the Chase Farm Hospital's high-security psychiatric ward, and had to pass through two iron gates before I could see the patient. After his emotions had calmed down, he confessed that he had hurt his girlfriend and felt very regretful. I tried to comfort him and left a copy of the Chinese newspaper "Tsing Tao Daily" with him before I said goodbye.

Chapter 19 Establishing Ministries

In 2006, I met a missionary couple from Hong Kong, Mr & Mrs Joe Tam. Being like-minded, we hit it off right away. I had great respect for their coming all the way to the UK to promote their ministry. They hoped to establish in London – in particular, near Chinatown where Chinese people gathered – a Chinese Christian Outreach and Resources Centre. The aim was to serve the Chinese community, especially in social care, in the spirit of Jesus' disciples and apostles' mission, live out the love of the Lord Jesus Christ, and to preach the gospel to the elderly. Joe originally founded The Media Evangelism Limited in Hong Kong, and brought many gospel videos to the UK. These would enable us to screen real-life stories that appealed to the elderly, to spread the gospel. I thought this was a good idea and agreed to help, and became their first co-worker, working together to establish the ministry.

Love is not caring about how we ourselves would benefit. Among faith, hope and love, love is the greatest. In order to build people up, believers must start with love. But we have to be prudent, everything requires patience, lest the gospel of Christ be blocked. After searching for more than six months, we found a building suitable for setting up the centre at the back of the Rhenish Church in Orange Street. This showed that God had already prepared an ideal place for us. The goal of edifying people is to preach the gospel and to strengthen the faith of believers. Our belief is that we should seek to benefit others, rather than to benefit ourselves. Our main concern is the benefits of the gospel. In the early days, I hosted the fellowship for the elderly – the "Golden Age Fellowship". I would watch the video once and write down the detailed plot and the issues that would arouse their interest. After the launch, the response was overwhelmingly positive and the fellowship lasted for three years.

The Chinese Christian Ministry Resource Centre assisted in establishing the UK branch of Global Enrichment Theological Seminary (GETS UK) in 2008. Initially, there were the advanced course for lay Christians and bachelor's degree theology course, which were taught by lecturers sent from the US. Three years later, a master's degree course was added, which ran for nine years. During this period, I helped as a volunteer in their bookkeeping and compiled their annual financial statements. The centre held an Alpha course in 2007 to help believers from the Lutheran Church to learn about God and be edified. In 2018 we held two evening Alpha courses for people to join after work. I was one of the facilitators.

In 2011, the centre started "Oasis in Chinatown" for the elderly. We helped them translate and fill out benefit application forms, held basic English classes (I helped as a substitute teacher). The visitors could read newspapers, play chess, enjoy the massage chair, and have their blood pressure checked. Free refreshments were available, and the service proved very popular with the elderly and restaurant workers during their afternoon break.

In 2013, I assisted in setting up the Holistic Good News Network (HGNN), which was officially established on June 1st that year. We collaborated with Our Daily Bread Ministries, and recorded materials from Our Daily Bread and the Discovery series for online broadcast in Mandarin and Cantonese. We also worked in conjunction with Herald UK, and recorded articles from their "Lifeline" and other columns for broadcasting online. I hosted a special programme for the network launch, in which I interviewed Dr Ho Wai Chu about her missionary trip to Africa.

From 2009 to 2019, the centre held the Living Water Fellowship, later renamed the Living Stones Fellowship. During this period, I hosted once a month, with the theme around the teachings of the Bible, supplemented with hymns, sometimes also with films or videos. We aimed to subtly instil the gospel message into participants, and countless people were moved to be baptised when their faith matured. They were then referred to a church of their choice. One of them was baptised at the centre by the retired Pastor Paul Chong.

Chapter 20 Life's Second Half

L ife is like a football match – it is difficult to predict the outcome until the final whistle. The gains and losses in the first half do not represent the results of the second half. Taking age as an example, some children die at a very young age, and some adults die of cancer in the prime of their life. Life's second half varies from person to person. If we assume our average age is eighty, then someone in their 40's would be in the second half of their life. I was born and raised in Hong Kong, my hometown. I was in my 50s when we migrated to the UK in 1995, so I was in the second half of my life.

In 1995 Angela and I came with our 12-year-old younger son, and stayed at a friend's place in south London. We stayed there for a week, then moved into a B&B. Before coming to the UK, Angela had secured a job with a British organisation and we had attended an exhibition in Hong Kong where UK properties were promoted and advertised. When we went to the London sales office of the same property developer, we found out that the show house was available for sale. We had a house viewing and decided to buy it. In addition to solving the problem of finding a new home for ourselves, it also allowed us to apply for a place at a local school for our son. Although Angela had to travel some distance to work, it was quite convenient to change trains on the London Underground. Newly built houses in England were usually sold without furniture or carpets, with no grass in the garden, but our show house had most of the things we needed, including cooking utensils, so we were really fortunate.

Having settled my wife and son, I went to the supermarket to purchase food and other basic household necessities, as well as canned food for emergencies. After my son was admitted to a school and my wife had settled into her job, I returned to Hong Kong to quit my job and sell our flat there. In the following year, I took our elder son, Mother and my mother-in-law to England to reunite with my wife and younger son. During my mother-in-law's stay with us, her brother, sister-in-law and their daughter from Norway came to visit us. They hadn't seen each other for many years, and it was a joy to see them re-united and pouring out their hearts to each other. Mother often went to the supermarket with my mother-in-law. Despite their not being able to speak or understand English, they were able to enjoy breakfast in the local restaurant without us having to worry about them getting lost. After a month's happy reunion, our sons had to go to school, and our respective mums sadly had to say goodbye to their grandchildren. We took the two of them to the airport, where the stewardess escorted them onto the plane to Hong Kong. There my younger siblings would pick them up on arrival.

After settling down in the UK, a friend referred me to a pastor. The pastor was a very approachable and soft-spoken man. He asked about our current situation and invited us to his church St Martin-in-the-Fields' Chinese service. The church is close to Chinatown, near Trafalgar Square in Westminster, opposite the National Gallery. This majestic building from the 17th century also houses the Ho Ming Wah Chinese Centre in the basement, and the Centre's location made it an ideal place for Chinese gatherings. We had no relatives or friends in the UK. His invitation enabled us to participate in Sunday worship, and to meet a group of Chinese brothers and sisters who love God and are eager to help others. It dispelled my doubts about emigrating and boosted my confidence in living in the UK. It seemed to be God's plan to lead our family to London. The Lord Jesus had not forgotten me, a prodigal son who had strayed from Christianity. I asked again and again: "Lord! You have helped my family adapt to London. If it pleases You, may You lead us forward so that all will go well."

God's mercy and kindness enabled me to realise my dream. With the recommendation of the pastor, I took a part-time job at the Ho Ming Wah Chinese Centre. In order to adapt to the British culture and integrate into the society, during lunch time, I would take my homemade sandwich and sit on a bench in the nearby park and chat with people in English to improve my listening and speaking skills. London is a world-renowned metropolis, with great heritage of western culture. It is also a centre of culture and entertainment, with museums, libraries, opera houses and theatres. It is indeed a place where our whole family can live and work in peace and contentment. It is my second home, and a home which I love.

Chapter 21 A Thunderbolt

As the university's final exams were approaching in May 2001, one night after midnight, the ringing phone woke me. When I picked it up, I heard my sister's frantic voice on the phone: "Mother had a heart attack! The doctors are now in the emergency room trying to save her. Can you come back to see her one last time?" The thunderbolt sent shock waves through my mind, like a thousand arrows piercing my heart. I replied in tears: "Please send me a certificate from the hospital so that I can apply for leave with the university." The next day my sister faxed over a hospital certificate. I immediately took it to the university and asked to defer my assignments and exams, not knowing when I was going to be able to graduate.

That evening on the direct flight to Hong Kong, I was filled with emotions. I dreamed of Mother's kind, frail face, her cheeks etched with wrinkles left over by years of hard work, lying on the hospital bed, motionless. I cried out: "God! Please shower my beloved mother with Your great love and mercy. May Your mighty hand heal her and restore her normal heartbeat. Allow me twelve more hours for my flight, so that I can see her one last time." God had heard and accepted the prayer in my dream. On arrival, I dropped my luggage at the family home and took a taxi to the hospital. There were tubes in Mother's nostrils and an oxygen mask over her mouth. Fortunately, her eyes were still slightly opened, and she saw that her son had returned. My eyes welled up but I had to hide the tears.

The next morning, my younger sister and younger brother rushed back from Canada and Australia respectively, and we all gathered to see the doctor in charge. He was direct with us: "The patient had a stroke and cerebral haemorrhage. Would you like me to operate on her? There may be complications during the operation, which may result in a lot of blood loss, and she may die immediately on the operating table." We discussed among ourselves and told him that we did not want to take the risk and asked him not to operate. The doctor replied, "In that case, you should prepare for the funeral."

In accordance with Mother's previous instructions, the family started preparing for the funeral. One day while I was at the hospital to visit her, I was surprised to find a small chapel in the hospital. Kneeling down reverently, I poured out my heart to God, asking him to soothe Mother's pain and let her pass away peacefully. After two weeks, Mother's condition gradually improved, and she was able to eat and get out of bed. One night, she went to the toilet on her own and fell over. It never rains but it pours: she broke her neck and had to wear a rubber brace to fix it. The fracture gave her excruciating pain. She kept asking for painkillers, but didn't take them right-away. Instead, she saved them up and tried to take them all in one go, hoping to end her suffering. Fortunately, a nurse discovered her plan in time and saved her life.

I waited and prayed for her to get better, and a month passed quickly. With God's help, Mother recovered gradually, except that her neck had not completely healed and she still needed to wear the rubber brace. As my siblings and I had rushed back from abroad, we all had work to do. After discussion, we agreed with family members in Hong Kong that the three of us would go home, and return for Mother's birthday in September. We hoped that she would recover in time and be discharged from hospital to recuperate at home.

On my return to the UK in early June, I rushed to the university to cancel my leave, and asked if I could take the exams as scheduled. The counsellor replied: "Originally you had two modules outstanding, but because you had extra lessons on one of the modules during the summer vacation and handed in your assignment, the professor has given you 20 credits and dispensed with the exam. You also handed in your assignment for the other module so only need to take one exam. There are two weeks left so you can take the exam." I passed the exam and was overjoyed. The three years of hard work had not gone to waste, and my life-long dream had been realised.

Chapter 22 After-Effects

One day during work at the Ho Ming Wah Chinese Centre, I had to open a folding table. As I bent down to lift the table, I suddenly heard a cracking sound from my lower back. Sensing something wrong, I sat down to rest, but it still hurt. Painkillers didn't help. Back home, I applied some traditional remedy, which did not work either. At that time, I had not registered with the National Health Service (NHS), nor did I have private health insurance. The pastor's wife introduced me to a private chiropractor, who offered me 50% discount. It took me four months of treatment to fully recover. Having learned my lesson, I bought medical insurance just in case such accidents should happen again. Six months later, I registered with the NHS. Worried about after-effects of the injury to my back, I got my family doctor to refer me to orthopaedics at the hospital.   After a CT scan, the consultant confirmed that I had osteoporosis and prescribed calcium tablets to prevent further bone degeneration. With physiotherapy and regular exercises, the pain gradually subsided and I didn't need any more painkillers.

I spent a lot of time in the university library. Day after day for long hours, I would read reference books, exhausting my eyes and causing fatigue. Without regular eye tests, I did not realise that my presbyopia was worsening, and that it was causing dry eyes and discomfort. The optometrist referred me to Moorfields Eye Hospital in London, a world-renowned eye hospital. In addition to treating patients, it had a research department and trained students to become specialist ophthalmologists. I usually had to wait for two to three hours each time, to be triaged and examined with advanced equipment. The eye drops and ointments prescribed by the doctor cured my symptoms. Grateful for the treatment I received, I joined the Moorfields Eye Hospital Charity as a patient member to help to raise awareness and promote their research and development fundraising campaigns.

It never rains but it pours. I developed irritable bowel syndrome (IBS), a common functional bowel disease with the main symptom being abdominal pain or discomfort. The dietician advised me to eat healthy meals every day to maintain a good-quality diet, and abstain from beans and dairy products. I have to avoid alcohol, coffee, tea with milk, pungent and fatty food. Instead, I need to eat lots of vegetables and fruits, and drink plenty of water. I exercise for half an hour every morning, and practice Tai Chi at home in the afternoon. Although I am a little thin, I feel relaxed when I exercise. It also reduces stress and is greatly beneficial to my health.

One day, my nose started to bleed continuously. I saw my family doctor, who suspected that my taking aspirin might be one of the reasons, and told me to temporarily stop taking it. The nosebleeds continued, however, so he referred me to an Ear, Nose and Throat specialist clinic. On examination, the consultant found that my nostrils were asymmetrical, resulting in the left nostril being overworked, and the veins therein prone to bleeding. He cauterised the veins and the bleeding stopped. However, I lost much of my sense of smell after the procedure – the gain is not worth the loss!

Chapter 23 Church Life

After migrating to the UK in 1996, we made London our home and attended the St Martin-in-the-Fields Chinese service every Sunday. The Chinese congregation was established in 1964 by their first pastor, Rev Lee Siu Ying. At the time, many Chinese were moving to the UK from Hong Kong and the New Territories. They were mostly engaged in the catering industry. Since the majority of them did not speak English, the Bishop Ho Ming Wah Chinese Centre was set up as an affiliate to the church to help them integrate into society. At Rev Gilbert Lee's invitation, our family attended their Sunday worship. They had youth and adult fellowships, so we were all happy to participate. After years of nurture and guidance from Rev Lee, Angela and I were baptised by him on 4 April 1999 and became Christians.

With the help of brothers and sisters in Christ, we quickly integrated into this big family. As a lay Christian, I was particularly interested in participating in the adult fellowship, and benefited much from the pursuit of biblical truth and brothers and sisters' sharing. Believers fellowshipped in God's love, and we experienced their heart-warming love and care for each other. The pastor's preaching, coupled with the Scripture of the day, shone a light on the truth of God's word for the whole congregation. In addition to the pastor's assistant reading the Call to Worship passage, the congregation would read the responsive Scripture together. All this was a very good worship procedure. The choir singing hymns and praises was an indispensable part of the worship. The congregation would join in with excitement and joy, offering praise to God.

Reading the Bible and praying at home are our homework. The Bible teaches us the desire to be like Jesus. I cannot do this on my own, but God has given us the Holy Spirit so that Christians can begin a life in Him and live out the image of His Son Jesus. When I pray, I am guided by the Holy Spirit to practice my spiritual life, and gradually grow. After the baptism, encouraged by brothers and sisters in the church, I began to lead the adult fellowship, and was selected as the head of the visitation team. I accompanied the pastor to visit other brothers and sisters in need, especially the sick and the elderly who were house-bound. This is in line with how much God cares about our lives. We laid hands on them and prayed for God's healing. We prayed in faith, believing that the Lord will heal them. Quiet time and devotional studies were also an integral part of personal spiritual practice and the joy of communicating with God.

I was elected a steward several times at annual church meetings, to assist the pastor in promoting church events and development. Among them was the 40th anniversary celebration of St Martin's Chinese Church. Guests were invited and those who were officiating delivered speeches. I was responsible for coordinating the commemorative magazine and inviting senior church members to contribute thanksgiving articles. It was a festive and joyful day, when church members gathered together in celebration.

Later when the church was rebuilt and repaired, leased stalls beside the church building had to close. Room was made through excavation for another floor to be built below to accommodate the large meeting hall of the Ho Ming Wah Chinese Centre on the bottom floor, while the middle floor was expanded for the shop where souvenirs were sold. As the church is a listed building, its exterior and interior could not be altered and could only be renovated. I was appointed as a member of the Rebuilding Committee. The project raised £32 million and the renovation was successfully completed.

Rev Li Tim-Oi was a pioneer in the movement to promote the ordination of female priests in the UK. She served as a pastor for 48 years and died in 1992 at the age of 85. To commemorate her, her family established the Li Tim-Oi Foundation to promote and subsidise the training of African women committed to becoming pastors, missionaries, parish administrators or school mentors. I was honoured to become one of the trustees of the Foundation.

Chapter 24 Long Journey To Realising My Mission

I n 2008, thanks to the love of our Heavenly Father, the calling of Lord Jesus, and being moved by the Holy spirit, I received the discipleship training in our church. If a Christian does not practice the Way, he would be self-righteous and arrogant. I must therefore fulfil the command of Lord Jesus' great commission in the Christian faith and devote my life to be a disciple of the Lord. My life had undergone a complete change: I became a new creation, putting myself in God's hands, letting Him shape me according to His will. From the heart, I had been wholly transformed by God, reborn into a new life, and became a disciple of Christ. I surrendered my will to God's sovereignty, and I obeyed and trusted Him completely. I have to admit that there were struggles during the spiritual journey, but in the end I obeyed God's will.

One day, I was alone with Rev John Yap, and he asked me directly: "I know you studied theology at the COCM Bible College. Have you considered taking it to the next level – undergo training from the parish in order to be accredited as a preacher on completion of the training?" I replied, "Can I? I'm already past my retirement age……" He said, "Why not? Only pastors have an age limit – and this is only because after training and ordination, pastors must serve in the parish for at least 10 years." Thanks to Pastor Yap's recommendation, I joined the "Faith and Worship" local preaching training. The course ran from September 2009 to

March 2013, followed by more than a year of preaching practice and assessments – and a final interview, which I passed. On 23 November 2014, I was officially accredited as a preacher.

I recall that at the beginning of my studies, I had to learn to write sermons and preach in class. Despite the teacher's instruction in the relevant unit of the course, he gave me a failing mark after I preached three times in front of my classmates as the audience. Later, during a summer retreat, I showed the first draft of my sermon to another teacher Rev Hazel Yu. After giving her comments, she told me to revise it. I returned to my room and worked until 3 am before showing her the revised draft later that day. Only then was it approved.

After my baptism, I was called by God three times to follow Him. To equip myself to become a useful vessel to Him, I joined the Local Preacher training. Since then, I had become more determined to serve the Lord. I remember the title of my first proper sermon was "Offering my best". I wanted to motivate myself to follow Christ's example of humility and love, to be His faithful servant. My motto is Psalm 61:8 "Then will I ever sing praise to Your name and fulfil my vows day after day".

After the first interview, my confidence in preaching and worship-leading grew with practice. The practice included writing sermons, preaching and leading worship. Through prayers, I was helped by the Holy Spirit. He enabled me to thoroughly understand the Scripture and accurately convey God's message. I could preach by explaining the Scripture, and applying the truth to the modern world and today's society. I applied biblical truths to real life stories, to spread the gospel and hopefully change the lives of the congregation.

I readily followed the circuit plan and church rota for preaching and worship-leading. My life was transformed. I regarded proclaiming and spreading the gospel as my mission – this was a heavy responsibility. After years of hard training, I had become a local preacher, and would make every effort to serve the congregation. This was a long journey to realising my mission. I would do my best whenever I preached or led worship, in the hope that the congregation would understand the message, remember it and practice it.

Chapter 25 Pastoral Co-Workers Coordinator

After working with Herald UK for many years, I was recommended by the Chairman of their Board of Directors to represent Herald UK in the Chinese Christian Co-workers Prayer Fellowship.   In 2013, I was unanimously approved to become the Fellowship's Coordinator for 2 years by their Selection Committee comprising Rev John Yap, COCM Representative Wang Guang Qi and Pastor Vincent Aun of the Chinese Church in London.

For each meeting, I would contact and consult pastors and preachers from churches in London and heads of Christian voluntary organisations, invite them to speak, introduce and promote their chosen topics, and draft up the agenda. Very often groups or individuals from all over the world would come to the UK on missionary trips. We took these precious opportunities to invite them to visit us, to introduce and promote their ministries, and explore opportunities for future cooperation. Many of them were interested in joining our prayer meetings as guest speakers. Prior to each meeting, I would print the agenda, organise refreshments, the signature book, guest badges, etc.   At the meeting, I would introduce the keynote speaker and apologise for those who couldn't attend, invite speakers to speak according to the schedule, and record the content of their speeches. Finally, we would share a meal and our fellowship. Afterwards I would email the draft minutes to the chairman for approval before distributing them to members.

During my tenure, it was felt that the Fellowship was limited to pastoral co-workers within London, and major cities outside London such as Manchester and Birmingham were not included. Moreover, missionary organisations as well as individuals from all over the world wanting to promote their missions to various parts of the UK had no way of contacting church leaders and other Christian voluntary agencies. It was therefore proposed to change the name of the Prayer Fellowship to the UK Chinese Christian Co-workers Association. I was responsible for drafting the charter and submitting it to the Executive Committee of Prayer Fellowship for approval.

At the last meeting before the end of my tenure, I combined the attendance records and minutes of meetings during the two years into a book, and submitted it to the Chairman, Pastor Vincent Aun. As a souvenir, Brother Wang Guang Qi very kindly presented to me a beautiful scroll of Chinese calligraphy, of which I was most appreciative: it was headed "God blesses", with one hundred different styles of the Chinese character "Blessings".

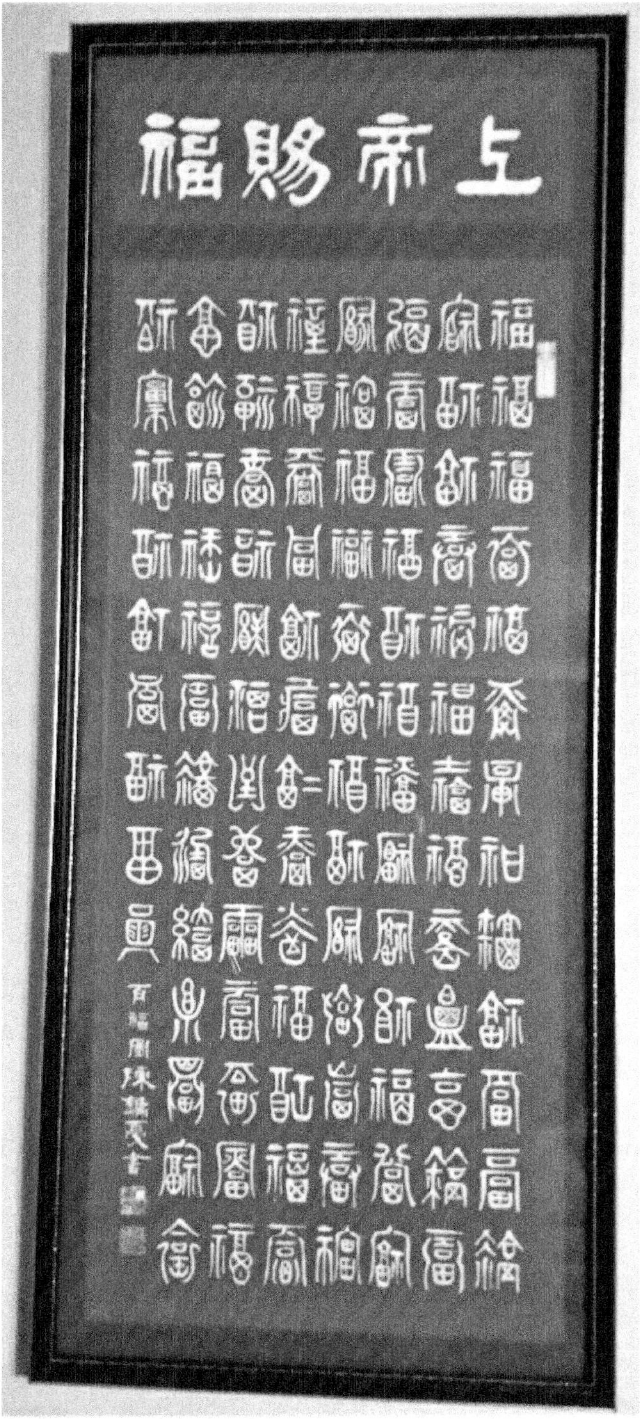
上帝賜福

Chapter 26 Journeying Through Life

J ourneying through life, we travel for many years, and everyone's experience is different. How do we know which is the right way when we navigate our own path of life? In particular, when we come to a crossroad, we look around but there are no directions, what do we do? Or, when travelling alone, with few people on the way whom we can ask for directions, how can we find our way to our destination?

When there seems no way out, don't be afraid. If we journey through life with a humble heart, there will be a way out. Every cloud has a silver lining. Some may say: "The roads are rugged and the mountain is steep. How do I make my way through this difficult journey? The following will help us navigate with courage through the difficult terrain:

Pause and rest awhile

When we lose our way, we become anxious. However, when we are tired from walking, we can stop, take a break, and rest awhile. Then, think about the next step, how to go forward. People often exhaust themselves trying to achieve goals beyond their ability, to the point of physical breakdown. We need to draw strength from our Heavenly Father, because those who look to the Lord will regain their strength; they will spread their wings and soar like eagles; they will run without getting weary, and walk without becoming exhausted.

Enjoy the scenery along the way

We work day and night, keeping ourselves busy. Take a holiday, and go away with your family or friends. Visit tourist attractions in the countryside, and you will find beautiful scenery of lakes and mountains. Listen to the birds sing, smell the fragrance of flowers in bloom. You will feel refreshed and revitalised, and feel like singing songs that praise God for creating the universe and the earth, such as " I lift up my Eyes to the Mountains ", "Flowers of the Field" and "Beauty of the Earth". Be amazed by the greatness of God's creation and the insignificance of man. And take the time to cherish our family and loved ones.

Review each stage of the journey

There are different stages in life, each stage with its own memories and recollections. Take time to reminisce. Savour the days of suffering, and how God has led us through them. Although we walk through the valley of the shadow of death, we are not afraid of being hurt, because God is with us; He is always comforting us. How bright and beautiful are the happy times! These are all gifts from God, as He has promised: "You will eat the fruit of your labour; blessings and prosperity will be yours."

Listen to God, walk with Him

We all know the story of Jesus calming the storm: the disciples' faith was tested and they came to realise how weak their faith was. When we walk with God, we should listen to His Word, so that He can guide and support us. He will point us to the road to blessings. With the faith to trust and obey, let us fix our eyes on Jesus, the author and perfecter of our faith. He is the Good Shepherd, and we will lack nothing. His rod and His staff will let us lie down in green pastures, and lead us beside quiet waters. He refreshes our soul, and guides us to the hope of eternal life.

Chapter 27 Following
The Lord For Life

I am a believer called by God, chosen by Him. Although in the past I had the opportunity to come into contact with Christianity, I hadn't built up a relationship with Jesus Christ, and had no God in my heart, and no hope of eternal life in this world. Now I am reconciled with Him, and become closer to Him. My mind has been transformed and I have found a new self. This new man was created in God's image, to imitate the Lord's righteousness and holiness.

When I accepted Jesus and became a Christian, I was determined to commit myself to follow Him and be the Lord's disciple for life. This determination, as well as complete obedience and trust in God, is enough to give me God's protection. I strive to pursue spiritual growth, trusting in the truth of the gospel of Jesus Christ so that I can be saved. God's redemptive grace is a gift, which I received by faith. I need to humbly learn His teachings, practise them and apply them in my life. I press on towards the goal to attain the prize for which God has called me heavenward in Christ Jesus.

I understand that, because there is certainty of salvation in believing in Jesus, my outlook on life is completely different from the world's pursuit of money, material possessions, kudos and status. I can be indifferent to fame and fortune, and endure temptation. Every day God provides nourishment and living water to satisfy my spiritual needs. Life after this rebirth is full of joy and peace in the heart. With the assurance of salvation, I feel tomorrow will be a better day. This new life comes from the rich grace of God, and in His grace I can find blessing upon blessing. This truth of eternal life is my ultimate goal, and reaching it is a continuous process of growth and life renewal, experiencing God's amazing grace over the course of my life journey.

In John 10:10, Jesus says: "*I have come that they may have life, and have it to the full.*" When we believe in the Lord, all His children can receive this full life. Therefore, we should not be overwhelmed by adversity. At any stage of our life: birth, old age, sickness, or death, we can come to God without fear, pour out our heart to Him, thank Him for His daily guidance in leading us towards where we should go. The pressures and sufferings in life are spiritual exercises that enable us to be blessed with the power of God, and experience His abundant grace.

I abide by this covenant prayer as my motto:

I am no longer my own but Yours.
Put me to what You will,
Rank me with whom You will;
Put me to doing, put me to suffering;
Let me be employed for You,
or laid aside for You,
exalted for You, or brought low for You;
Let me be full, let me be empty,
Let me have all things,
Let me have nothing:
I freely and wholeheartedly yield all things
to Your pleasure and disposal.
So be it.
And now, glorious and blessed God,
Father, Son and Holy Spirit,
You are mine and I am Yours.
And the covenant now made on earth,
let it be ratified in heaven.
Amen !

Chapter 28 The Wonderful Life

When we evaluate our own life, we will realise how different we are from others – I am me, my body and soul are unique. Standing in the present and looking back at the past leaves one with many questions. Have I wasted my time? What am I living for? What is the meaning and value of life? I believe that no matter what the answer is, we cherish our lives and desire to live life to the full.

How can we achieve that? This is indeed a question that cannot be ignored. Many people may think that it would be nice to be like Prince William - born in the royal family, being second in the line of succession to the British throne, married to a beautiful wife, having a happy family, representing the royal family everywhere as a goodwill ambassador, popular and given VIP treatment wherever he goes, etc.

Can this identity as second in the line of succession to the throne guarantee a wonderful life? A wonderful life is not based on prominent lineage, dazzling wealth, a happy family, or celebrity status. The real brilliance lies in a heart content in all aspects. American business magnate and software developer Bill Gates is a good example. As of 2007, Bill and his wife Melinda Gates were the second-most generous philanthropists in America, having given over $28 billion to charity. The Bill and Melinda Gates Foundation supports, among other things, a wide range of public health projects, granting aid to widespread vaccine programmes to eradicate polio, as well as to fight transmissible diseases such

AIDS, tuberculosis and malaria. It grants funds to learning institutes and libraries and supports scholarships at universities. The foundation also established a water and hygiene programme to provide sustainable sanitation services in poor countries.

If we can avoid conforming to the worldly view in our pursuit of life, we will understand that wealth and status are fleeting and temporal. With peace of mind, we can be poor yet happy. In the Lord's Prayer, Jesus taught us to pray "Give us this day our daily bread". The truth is: God will provide what we need today, and we don't need to worry about tomorrow.

Jesus also taught us: first seek God's kingdom and His righteousness, and everything else will be given to us. As we journey through life with God, we can communicate with Him through reading the Bible, praying and meditating, let His truth shape our temperament and lead our life. In the spiritual world, God wants to broaden our horizon, enlighten our hearts, and allow our spirits to grow and be renewed every day, so we can gradually mature and bear the fruit of life. If we aspire to follow Jesus, we will know that He has sent His Spirit to dwell in the hearts of His believers, so that we can live in His love every day, live out His likeness, glorify God and be of benefit to others. This is what a wonderful life is all about.

Chapter 29 Marathon Of Life

T rack and field running can be roughly divided into sprint, middle-distance and long-distance running: 400 meters or below are sprints, middle-distance from 800 meters, and long-distance running from 3,000 meters. The marathon race is longer than 10,000 meters and is usually held on roads or highways, with crowds of onlookers waving flags, clapping, and cheering the athletes on until they reach the finishing line.

The Olympic records show that in the 400-metre race in Barcelona, Spain in 1992, British track and field athlete Derek Redmond suddenly had a torn right hamstring during the preliminaries. The pain was excruciating but he was determined to continue. Limping, he strained every sinew in a desperate effort to complete the race. His father Jimmy Redmond saw this, and before anyone could stop him, he quickly jumped over the fence and ran to his son. The son leaned on his father's shoulder, and hobbled through the remainder of the course. Seeing this, the spectators stood up and cheered the two men on. When they crossed the finishing line, it was as if all the spectators completed the race with them.

The same is true for the race in life. It's a long race. We are rushed through kindergarten, primary school, secondary school and university. After graduating from university, we enter the second stage of our lives: employment, setting up business, starting a family, and having children. Not every young person has the opportunity to progress to secondary school or university. One student I know had to drop out of primary school due to poverty. There were times when he stumbled and failed. Fortunately, he had been equipped with the Christian faith since his childhood. He believed that our Heavenly Father, who is sovereign in every difficult situation, would protect him and would never abandon His son, but help him as he journeyed through life.

When we are young, we often receive wedding invitations from former classmates, colleagues at work, and friends. In our twilight years, however, we tend to get news of elderly relatives and friends passing away. Such is life: there's a time for everything, a time to be born and a time to die. In life, everyone eats and drinks, and enjoys himself in all his toil. This is a gift from God, but people still don't realise God's deeds from beginning to end so that they can have a good life.

As the population continues to age, people's life expectancy is generally getting longer. When people enter old age, they will ask: where will we end up? A dying patient asked the pastor who came to visit him, "Pastor, where will my soul go after death?" The pastor replied, "Let us throw off everything that hinders and the sin that so easily entangles. And let us run with perseverance the race marked out for us, fixing our eyes on Jesus, the pioneer and perfecter of faith." When we follow Christ closely, our lives will be filled with a great sense of satisfaction, strong and lasting, surpassing all the riches, fame and status of this world. We firmly believe that our lives depend on God, and we should be strong and courageous! Don't be afraid, don't panic, because no matter where we go, God will be with us.

Chapter 30 God's Goodwill Over The Course Of My Life

As the saying goes: "Man proposes, God disposes". Of this, I have had profound experience.

In the fifties, I returned to Hong Kong to study at the age of nine. I set foot on Luohu Bridge alone and returned to Hong Kong to reunite with my father. Entering primary school as a newcomer in a strange land, I found it hard to catch up in the English class. Thankfully I was doing better in less than a year and got Grade A in Chinese, English and Mathematics in the Primary School Certificate Examination. I was overjoyed.

Heavy Blow - First Setback

With my excellent grades received in the Primary School Certificate Examination, I was accepted by the two prestigious English schools I applied for that year. However, there were hungry mouths that needed to be fed in the family. Big Aunt refused to let me go to either of these schools, and forced me to attend a lower secondary school run by a charity. As a twelve-year-old, I had no means of resisting this. When I graduated from lower secondary school at the age of fifteen, Father told me to follow in his footsteps and inherit his skills as a chef. At that age, I already knew how valuable education is, and I didn't give in. I told him that I didn't need his money and would pay for my own studies. Fortunately, he took on another apprentice and didn't pressure me anymore.

Self-Financing My Further Studies

Immediately I put my words into action, and sought to finance my studies. God didn't let me down: a newspaper publisher organised charitable grants for which students in poverty could apply. I went out at 4 am to queue up outside the newspaper office to obtain an application form. Fortunately, based on my family situation and good academic results, and my stated desire to complete the remaining three years of secondary education, they approved my application so I could do it in a prestigious Chinese secondary school. It is a Christian school, with a pastor teaching Bible studies. All students met in the auditorium every Monday morning for a worship session.

Stepping into Society, Earning a living and Supporting My Family

After graduating from secondary school at the age of nineteen, my aging father was diagnosed with cancer. As the eldest son, I shouldered the responsibility of looking after the family. Sadly in the 1960s, salaries in Hong Kong were meagre. Starting as a primary school teacher, I had to teach in the morning and evening to pay for my younger siblings' education. Later I changed my career and became an audit clerk in an audit firm, and pursued further professional studies for self-improvement. I could only envy all my classmates who went to university. Times were tough; I dreamt of one day being able to study at a university. In particular, I dreamt of studying at a university in the UK, because British universities had a good reputation. I even bought a book entitled "How to get a degree in Britain?"

A Dream Come True

My long-time hope was realized in 1996 when we made London our home. When I first arrived in the UK, I couldn't understand the locals' English accent or read the newspapers. So I went to a college to study "English for Speakers of Other Languages" for two and a half years. One day, the teacher asked me if I had thought of going to university. I replied: "This is my dream and plan." So in 1998, under his guidance, I realised my wish to go to university, and obtained a bachelor's degree in psychology in 2001.

Believing in Jesus and being Baptised

At Easter in April 1999, not only did I get to know Jesus, I also accepted Him as my Saviour. My wife and I were baptised and became His children in the name of the Lord. Jesus chose us and we became Christians. He also gave us the gifts to serve him: we both serve with the Herald Christian paper. We have accepted His call to glorify His name. Looking back on my life, if I hadn't studied Chinese in secondary school, I might not have the skills and knowledge required to read and write like I do today. After graduating from university, I studied theology and became a preacher. In the Bible, Proverbs 16:9 has a clear lesson: *"In his heart a man plans his course, but the Lord determines his steps."* I can see God's goodwill over the course of my life. With gratitude, I offer my body as a living sacrifice. I vow to God: "Abba Father, I am willing to offer the rest of my life for Your use. May it be pleasing in Your sight!"

ABOUT THE AUTHOR

Alan Tak Ming Lun

Alan Tak Ming Lun was born in Hong Kong in 1944, and experienced World War II. Coming from a working-class family, he has always enjoyed reading and writing as his hobbies and habits. He joined the Christian publication "Herald" more than 20 years ago, and is now on the Monthly Special Topic Design Team. He contributes to the "Melody of Life" column under the name "Lun Tak Ming"; the "Lifeline" column under the pen-name "Sun, Moon & Stars"; the "Monthly Special Topic" column under the pen-name "The Observer"; and the "Featured article" column under the pen names "In Turn" and "Self-Starter".

Under God's guidance, he came to the UK in 1995, and was able to go to university. He obtained a bachelor's degree in psychology in 2001, and became a member of the British Psychological Society. He then graduated from COCM Bible College, and took elective courses at GETSUK Theological Seminary. After completing a preaching course from the parish, he became a servant of the Lord – a lay preacher.

Now in his retirement, he still enjoys writing, and is thankful to be able to realise his long-time dream of publishing his first book. Previously, he contributed an article "London: My Second Home" under the pen-name "Jiaxing" to a book entitled "Yesterday Remembered". This was a collection of short essays and poems by Chinese Londoners.

Printed in Great Britain
by Amazon